WHAT THE AI

A Journey Through the Rise and Impact of Artificial Intelligence

Mian Khan

Contents

1

INTRODUCTION

How do you think Siri or Alexa can converse with us as though that is the only thing they do all day? Or stand as the masters of our smart houses and computers, easing us into our everyday lives? Right from unlocking our cell phones using face recognition through biometric systems for identity verification to self-driving vehicles while in traffic, they all have one reason lying behind this revolution, Artificial Intelligence (AI)

AI essentially provides smart/intelligent machines with the ability to think and perform tasks, which are typically considered a domain only for humans as it involves accepting and performing complex activities. But really, how did we arrive at the threshold and what are the implications in the future for this generation? This story follows the rise of AI, its sociological impact, and the moral dilemmas that we are falling into in this age of fast-paced change.

This is a future wherein your virtual assistant understands your routine more than you do, your house can change these temperatures and the amount of light depending on the preference you have without lifting a finger and your car drives itself amid heavy traffic in the city. All these can be done as a result of one technology which is regarded as being fundamental. This is artificial intelligence (AI). From the idea of just talking through devices to employing self-driven cars, AI is the driving force behind the next generation of technology.

AI allows machines to execute tasks that were previously thought to be unattainable, emulating human capabilities in ways that were once considered to be the stuff of fiction. This book examines the historical emergence of AI as well as its stunning effects and the challenges generated by its endless progress in terms of morality.

2

The Rise of ChatGPT & Everyday AI

J ust weeks after its release, ChatGPT took over the scene, establishing a new horizon for the relationship between humans and machines." ChatGPT was launched in November 2022 and rightly went viral due to the ridiculously fast growth to 100 million active users. This was not an ordinary gadget; it was more like a virtual assistant who organized calendars, set notifications, planned events, and composed songs or films.

This unprecedented growth marked a new intersection in human-machine interaction, but it brought about challenges as well. They used ChatGPT for different reasons which included guiding them through a meditation session or helping them organize the recipes. It became apparent that this was no longer a device for amusement but one that improved aspects of daily living and as a result, created a huge buzz and concern on how this would affect people who would with the AI for tedious activities.

ChatGPT was made different from the usual AI tools because of its conversational manner. Unlike Google or other AI who can be commanded to do one particular task, ChatGPT could respond to queries, partake in dialogue, and produce human mimic content. This capability of comprehension or 'what we see in movies quickly and easily shocked many millions of people who transformed it from a toy into an everyday requirement to most people.

AI's Legal and Ethical Challenges

The introduction of ChatGPT was one of the most notable advancements in AI technology as it altered how people approached technology. Debuted in November 2022, ChatGPT hit the roof at record speed, having over 100 million users within just a few months, making it the fastest growing App in the history of technology. It was not a normal bot; ChatGPT was a bot that almost felt human and could hold a conversation, respond to questions, write articles, and give out recommendations.

For all the fun that it could provide, ChatGPT was about more than just entertainment. People started using it for organizing their work, setting up appointments, and even composing songs or writing stories. The AI's ability to engage in conversation without strange pauses or disjointed thoughts and handle narrative relevance did not help matters either as the AI ceased to become a tool but rather morphed into a companion for most users. This outbreak of popularity demonstrated once again what possibilities AI can open up for personal productivity. However, Scipion's warning was uncomfortably prophetic – it also revealed the increasing reliance on technology.

The launch of the GPT store by OpenAI in January 2024, altered the course of the AI industry relevance significantly. Then, it became possible to interact with a broader range of functionalities from within GPT without requiring third-party apps, thus changing the tech ecosystem. The hundreds of AI companies that relied on the At OpenAI APIs were also in dire straits, suggesting the might that one single entity in the AI industry could possess.

Launched in a manner that promised to address the concerns of the target users, the GPT store and such features, made irrelevant the need for a great number of third-party applications transforming the way users viewed AI-powered businesses. This conception proved catastrophic for most of the people who had come up with models 'on top' of OpenAI as they found themselves battling with the very platform that crowdfunded their applications, thus demonstrating the chaos of the AI business.

3

Deepfakes

Much as the age of artificial intelligence progressed, an unfortunate shadow came into the picture. Being alarmed by the potential of deepfake technology, people began to realize how it was majorly blurring the line between fiction and reality. Deepfakes are one of many applications of AI that create highly sophisticated computer-generated videos deepfakes that have raised Pandora's box of worries about misinformation, impersonation, and political interference.

Deep fakes have been employed to manufacture fake news, modify statements, and impersonate people to a level that appears real. As these weapons of mass deception become more democratized, Layton predicts a scenario where it will be next to impossible to tell real from doctored content. Such dissemination of the painful reality dictates the clear call of such soft powers as ethical codes and legal reinforcement to avoid bad scenarios from happening. The sweetening mixture of these hyper-realistic altered videos is that such videos will be able to encapsulate faces, voices, and actions in a way that fake content will be illuminating freshness rather than draining it. The dark side of AI which distorts reality using technology became associated with Deepfakes in no time at all.

However, these painless and explicable solutions need an internalization of certain AKP frameworks before that potential, self-inflicted danger becomes real.

The very deepfake ethical issues are not limited to politics. Deepfakes threaten privacy and identity on an individual basis because someone can create a deepfake of you and use it for impersonation to either make quick money or use it to ruin your name. Deepfakes are increasingly common, therefore, the need for measures to regulate and control their negative effects is long overdue.

Internal Struggles and Strategic Shifts at OpenAI

Despite its achievements, OpenAI encountered some internal problems that revealed how complicated it is still to fit into the context of the rapidly developing AI industry. In late 2023, OpenAI's head Sam Altman was unceremoniously ousted as CEO with no commercial consensus about core strategies. Proponents of AI industry turned out to be also fans of constant conflicts, and a lot of complexity lay in the center of managing a cutting-edge AI company.

Ethical issues, the proper course of AI enhancement, and the issues concerning the consequences of AI technologies on humanity itself became sources of tension within Open AI. Any peaceful exit of Altman underscores that commonly known internal issues even the dominant tech actors face should be put aside for achievement with a focus on the most disturbing technologies accessible by humanity.

There was another noteworthy aspect of the management reshuffle in OpenAI: No one seems to be saying that there is a fair delineation of equitable boundaries of AI ethics. As these types of AI systems develop further in complexity and capabilities so will the sheer power of those that lead the companies behind them, and how they will shape the future of technology - and hence the world.

Deepfakes are dangerous for democracy anyway and are even more of a problem in politics. Take, for instance, a situation in which a certain politician gets his or her speech edited so that the politician's view on an important matter bears a different look, or the photo of a certain world leader is altered in the light of a suggestive controversy. Such fraudulent material would mislead the electorate, tampering with the electoral processes, and in the process, undermining governments. This makes the debate on deepfakes and their possible implications more complex as their threat is on the rise and tackling it will require all the efforts of technologists, politicians, and society.

Changes in AI have, however, not been without some within-wars. In 2023, Sam Altman opened a new chapter with Mitsubishi Corporation, notwithstanding the ongoing governance differences; he was already in impact as the CEO of Forma since 2021. Following this departure, OpenAI's internal climate changed dramatically, and the Central strategies of the company and its further movement were already in the spotlight discussions. More so as OpenAI has managed to break taboos, the issue of who wields this powerful instrument and steers it appeared more pressing than ever.

The uproar regarding Altman's removal revealed the struggles within the administration of AI development when creativity is at odds with ethics. Being an active leader in AI development, OpenAI started to receive criticism about the application of its technologies. Such internal debates regarding data protection, discrimination of algorithms, abuse of AI systems, and many other concerns sparked controversy within the organization and eventually led to leadership upheavals that revealed the hurdles associated with the management of AI going forward.

Global AI Race: The Rise of China's Kuo and Cling

Yet, if OpenAI appeared to command global coverage, China was not far behind in emerging technologies. Surprisingly, Chinese firm Kuo created an advanced AI model called Cling, a video generation platform that quickly turned heads. Cling was a great leap in the AIs' ability as it could produce videos that were realistic from just a few words. What was more interesting was that Cling encouraged an open approach to its users to try out its technology, unlike other models that embraced more conservative policies. This brand of activity marked a radical change in the AI order globally as China continued to sink a lot of resources into developing AI tools to emerge as an authority in the discipline. The capabilities of Cling in generating spectacular videos also revealed China's technological capabilities and suggested a possible reorientation of AI power in the East.

The offer of Cling rounded and completed not only China's picture of success but, importantly, raised the topic of the race for AI. There is a growing scramble by nations for control in this changing environment and warfare begins with technology but spreads to other domains including but not limited to politics and economy as well as culture.

4

AI AND EMPLOYMENT

As AI technologies advanced at an unprecedented pace, concerns about job displacement began to grow. By 2024, the U.S. unemployment rate rose to 4.1%, partly driven by AI-induced job losses. Automation replaced roles traditionally filled by humans, from manufacturing and logistics to administrative tasks and customer service.

The fear of job displacement due to AI is not unfounded. As machines become capable of performing tasks once reserved for people, millions of jobs are at risk. However, the rise of AI also presents opportunities for new job creation in fields such as AI development, data science, and robotics. The challenge lies in equipping the workforce with the skills needed to thrive in this new landscape.

While AI's potential to automate tasks poses a threat to existing jobs, it also offers the chance to redefine work. Automation can take over repetitive, mundane, and hazardous tasks, freeing humans to focus on more creative, strategic, and empathetic roles. To navigate this transition, a concerted effort is needed to reskill workers and prepare future generations for a world where AI plays an integral role in the economy.

The competition between Cling and OpenAI's anticipated Sora model highlighted the global race to dominate AI development. Cling's open access allowed more people to experiment with its technology, setting it apart from other, more restricted models. This innovation, combined with China's broader ambitions in AI, suggests that the future of artificial intelligence will be shaped by a complex interplay of international forces.

Cling's success has also raised questions about data sovereignty and technological dominance. As AI models become more advanced, the data they are trained on plays a crucial role in shaping their behavior and output.

AI and Employment: Job Displacement and New Opportunities

The ethical rules, regulations, and organizational structures imposed on advanced AI systems became the prime area of concern. As of 2024, the U.S. unemployment rate stood at 4. An increasing number of automation and AI-developed systems created employment opportunities. The argument, however, was what economy will be created in its place and if any retraining programs for the displaced employees are required.

Employment from the side of AI is both a relief and a curse. Its advantage may be substituting the dull and hazardous forms of work and increasing the efficiency of industries. But this also endangers jobs from manufacturing to call centers. It is understood that as AI comes closer to human consciousness, millions of employment opportunities will be in danger. This compels, once more, a complete reform of the policy on the workforce and the educational system. Cling's open access friend not contrary to the trend towards initial enthusiasm for its technology enabled the kill of more users and organized on controlling it. This in particular the bonanza of AI tools characterized an even bigger change throughout the world the need comprehended by China has been larped out. Noticeable video-making prowess from Cling showcased the kind of technological capabilities developing in China suggesting that the lead of AI development may gravitate east in the coming years.

The launch of Cling brought to light the Chinese developments and it also raised the issues of the global race for the AI sector. The developments in various countries towards a leading position in this new area stretch way beyond the technology level and seep into the realm of politics, economy, and culture.

Concerns regarding job loss began to increase as the developments in AI technologies increased by leaps and bounds. A portion of the rise in US unemployment, which reached 4.1% in 2024, was attributed to artificial intelligence-related job cuts. As time went on, machines took over the tasks of operations in sectors such as manufacturing, logistics, administration, customer service, and others that were run by people.

Fears related to AI are very much justified when it comes to job loss due to the effect of AI. Many workers will be displaced because the work that humans used to do will be accomplished by machines. However, the emergence of AI also comes with the advantages of creating jobs within AI development, data analysis, and robotics. The difficulty however is on how to prepare the workers to match with the competencies required in that new or changed environment.

This competition of sorts for attention from the workers in those industries has induced, and in a way decreased, the belief that these changes in work could be as radical as the changes in the office with the advent of new communication technology. But while some jobs are eliminated by AI, others become available. For example, AI, robotics, and data science ascend with plenty of opportunities available that did not exist ten years ago. The problem is how this shift is to be managed so that society adjusts to what AI has to offer with regard to work approaches but at the same time minimizes the downsides that are associated with employability.

5

THE HUMAN ELEMENT

Also, AI has shown its usefulness in healthcare amid these changes. For instance, Powerly AI provides AI services for Alzheimer's and dementia patients through chatbots to help them keep memories and bond with family. This novel application of the AI brandishes the constructive impact the technology has on the people as never seen before.

Such AI-based applications provide supportive care for individuals with cognitive impairment such as reminding them, accompanying them, and providing them with cognitive tasks. These patients and caregivers find relief when using these artificial conversational agents because the agents record their memories and play them back to the patients.

As a further instance, Neuralink, founded by Elon Musk, allows the first patient to walk thanks to a special device and AI technologies, demonstrating a unique ability for the application of such AI solutions. Through the connection of brain messages and movement, these AI devices that are implanted in an awfully sick but soon-to-be healthy individual are providing new hope in the treatment of paralysis and other brain illnesses.

The Journey of AI: From Early Concepts to Modern Marvels

In order to grasp the significance of present-day AI, one has to delve into its history. Constructing intelligent machines is an endeavor that can be traced to ancient societies, but such aspiration is assumed science around the twentieth century. Many people regard Alan Turing as the father of artificial intelligence among others because of the importance of his efforts right from its inception. For instance, his contribution to the Turing Test was critical in offering machine intelligence with one of its first quantifiable parameters.

The imagination of Turing where a human brain can be incorporated within a machine was a new idea. It was to trigger years of research and invention. From the simple maze-solving program of the 1950s to how it is today where solace is found in powerful artificial neural networks, a lot has happened in the terrain called artificial intelligence that at its dawn even the founders of the field could not have imagined.

AI today can recognize objects from photographs, produce text, and even design realistic graphics based on elaborate descriptions.

6

CONCLUSION

It is well known that today, AI has taken over every aspect of our daily lives, including what we purchase and how we connect with each other. Experts contend that in a few decades, artificial intelligence could be so developed that it surpasses the capabilities possessed by human beings leading to another phase of the development in technology. This would start those much-needed advanced regimes that would transform the way society features from eradicating diseases to overcoming intricate issues on an international level.

As the author Joanna Maciejewska expressed, I want AI to handle tasks like laundry and dishes, freeing me to focus on writing. Drones have become popular over the past five years, yet restrictions and delays in regulations hinder their potential use in firefighting and rescue missions. It's frustrating that the same drones we play with could be saving lives, spraying water, or extinguishing fires. As AI continues to replace jobs, many will evolve rather than disappear, much like the shift from outdated jobs in the 1900s. However, the transition will be tough, with job loss before we adapt to mastering AI. Eventually, we will catch up, and looking back, we'll appreciate the progress. Nevertheless, that change will take place, and indeed there will be downsizing coming before we understand how to acclimate to the efficient use of AI. In the end, fortunately, we will be able to reach that point where we will look back and sigh appreciation for the developments that have been made.

Nonetheless, it is said that great power calls for great responsibility. Decisions taken today in terms of developing, governing, or embedding Auxiliary Intelligence will have future implications like none before. We are on the threshold of a new age when machines will impact all facets of society toward becoming more automatons. Though the fans and the future might be Athena-bright, society, and the right will have to take an active role in shaping the future of things in this ominous world of great possibilities.

7

THANK YOU

Dear Reader,

Thank you so much for taking the time to read my book. Your support and interest mean the world to me. I hope you found it enjoyable, insightful, and perhaps even inspiring. Your journey through these pages is greatly appreciated, and I am truly grateful for your readership.

With heartfelt thanks,

Mian Khan

www.ingramcontent.com/pod-product-compliance
Lightning Source LLC
LaVergne TN
LVHW051651050326
832903LV00034B/4817